GOING UP!

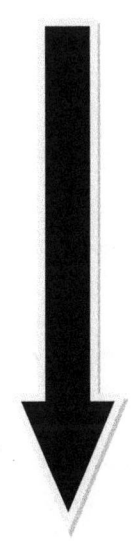

GOING UP!

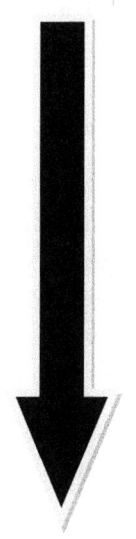

Dr. C.J. Staton

Copyright ©2019 Dr. C.J. Staton

All Rights Reserved.

Printed in the United States of America

Editor: LPW Editing & Consulting Services, LLC
www.litapward.com

Cover Design: Dr. Frederick Best, *Born 2 Win*

First Printing, 2019

ISBN-13: 978-0-578-47168-6

No part of this publication may be reproduced, stored in a retrieval system, or transmitted in any form by any means, electronic, mechanical, photocopying, recording, scanning or otherwise, except as permitted under Section 107 or 108 of the 1976 United States Copyright Act, without the prior written permission of the author. Except in the case of brief quotations embodied in critical articles and reviews.

Scripture quotations are taken from the Holy Bible, King James Translation unless otherwise quoted.

Ordering Information: Books may be purchased in quantity and/or special sales by emailing Dr. Staton at statoncliff@yahoo.com.

Table of Contents

	Dedication	vi
	Foreword	viii
	Introduction	1
1	The Damascus Experience	3
2	Your Afflictions	9
3	Allow Patience to Work	15
4	Reality Check	19
5	Humility = Obedience	25
6	Pride ≠ Humility	31
7	Submit	33
8	The Choice is Yours	37
9	Don't Fool Yourself	41
10	The Secret to Greatness	47
11	Mirror or Window	51
12	Where Do You Stand	55
	About the Author	61

Dedication

To my lovely wife, Paulette, one of those good and perfect gifts that has come from above and has fallen to me. It is my hope that you will continue to manifest the full glory of God and allow the world around you to be blessed by your beautiful and Godly nature. You hunger and tenacity for God is my inspiration and I'm persuaded that those who will come in contact with you, will leave and never forget your beautiful smile.

To my beloved children, Clifton, Terrell, and Chantel, who have grown into three of the finest adults that two parents could ask for. Through the talents, abilities and gifting that God has filled your lives, I cannot forget your labor of love each of you have shared with me in ministry. I must warn those around you and the world that your fullest potential has not yet been revealed. And as a proud dad, I know that you guys will be making your marks as you continue to go through life acknowledging the God of Glory as your God. Always remember and never doubt your ability to achieve every goal that you will dare set in life. May your generation be the witness to your full glory.

Foreword

Oh how my heart burns it is finally here God has released a fresh revelation in the heart of this great man, Bishop Clifton Staton. A revelation to this existing generation and to the past generations and generations to come. Many Christian people have failed to understand the true process and what it truly takes to arise to your destiny. The revelation of the destine calling, which is the Lord Jesus Christ who is the system that God has designed to get us to our destiny, many people in the body of Christ have abandon that system trying to come up with their own way to arise to success. Isn't it strange how many young people are trying to thrust themselves into ministry without learning the revelation of serving. How can you truly become a minister in the gospel if you have not became a servant in the house. Yes indeed God has always used the process of humility in order to lift us up into our ministry or calling.

This is a unique, revelational book, and it is a must have. If you do not get this book in your library and understand the revelation of this book you can find your bookshelf quite empty even if you have a thousand books on your bookshelf. If you don't understand the revelation of humility, it is humility that gives each one of your books the power to help push you into your destiny. It is amazing how Saul of Tarsus thought that he was powerful because he went to the most educated school, set under the world greatest mind, it wasn't until he had a Damascus experience that he realize how little he knew. For some of us God is taking us through a strip away season, it is not a season to destroy us it is a season to destroy that which wants to hold on to you, that would have the power to destroy you. You can only arise through this season by embracing the spirit of humility. I don't care how many times you're falling down humility is your way up. I don't care how hi your mountaintop experience maybe, you still have to complete the classroom of the valley. I am so grateful that God has sent us His manservant so that we can have an opportunity to have a teacher that will walk with us through the Word of God to get us to the mountaintop. You have indeed grabbed hold of one of the world's greatest book that would help you become what God has called you to be.

Thank you again Bishop Clifton Staton, I know you had to go down to the door way of revelation to invoke such a powerful revelation of humility. I am so honored to be a part of this process for I am embracing my Valley experience of humility, so like Caleb I can possess my mountain. Yes, give me my mountain through the doorway of humility!

Dr. Apostle Frederick R. Best
Founder & Sr. Pastor of
Unveiling Glory in Worship Ministry

Introduction

God's system of promotion is very unique and tempts us to abandon His process of getting us to the next place in life. God uses the process of humility just to lift us up. We all know that God is without limits and where He can take us is beyond that. But the mystery and key to getting into that upward process is by going down. And because of that, all of us have had our "Damascus Experience;" finding ourselves having to trust the process and the people who God have set in place for our lives. Purposely, He put us into a position and caused us to partake in the patience process. While He is working, we are forced to wait until the process has ended. And it is at this point, we are forced to face the reality. We are not God and we don't have the power to change things, people and not even ourselves!

We have to humble ourselves and call on a powerful, majestic and overwhelming God Who is able to deliver the righteous from his afflictions. Once more, it is at this point we must choose to obey God and walk in a spirit of humility. We have to acknowledge that we must reach a place where we can offer God the one thing that He did not give to us…Humility. Everything we give God, even our sacrifices, we are only giving back to Him what he has given unto us, but our humility and obedience are the things we can give to Him that He did not give to us. It's our choice. What this book does is it will force you to acknowledge whether your standing at the cross or kneeling at the cross.

HUMBLE YOURSELF AND BE LIFTED!

Chapter One

Your Damascus Experience

As we enter into the mind of God through His Word, we will find that every Word was set in its order with a masterly skill, proving the very competency of God. That He is more than sufficient to complete the work that was started in us. God's Word is the masterpiece that is able to bring us into the knowledge of knowing that we are deprived and corrupt. And outside of Him and being disconnected from Him, we are just ruined creatures. It is evident that we are wretched and need a Savior every time our minds meet our will and we end up in the struggle to yield ourselves to God. Therefore, it is expedient for us to get a daily dose of God's Word and look at the reflection of who it is that God wants us to become and what it is that He thinks of us as His prized creation.

If we will get a daily dose and allow ourselves to look into the reflecting mirror of His Word, we can see exactly who we are. One context said that without this same Word, not anything that was made would have been made. And what that gives us confidence in is that that same Word has the ability to transition us and cause us to operate at our highest level. But in order to operate at our highest level, a simple act of humility is all that is required from us. When we love God and do not learn the art of submission, then we find ourselves forced by our own will into a situation that will prompt us or immediately deliver us into a position of humility, even when we did not intend to put ourselves there. I call those situations our "Damascus Experiences." It's that situation where you had your own ideas, you had already made your plans, and you had already decided on how you would deal with your next situation. And without knowing and any intentions, we find ourselves down and looking up to God. It is at this point, God without our permission interferes, causing you to be knocked off the course you were on, and while there, your will is put under pressure until it is forced to surrender and submit.

Acts 9:1-6..."And Saul, yet breathing out threatenings and slaughter against the disciples of the Lord, went unto the high priest, And desired of him letters to Damascus to the synagogues, that if he found any of this way, whether they were men or women, he might bring them bound unto Jerusalem. And as he journeyed, he came near Damascus: and suddenly there shined round about him a light from heaven: And he fell to the earth, and heard a voice saying unto him, Saul, Saul, why persecutest thou me? And he said, Who art thou, Lord? And the Lord said, I am Jesus whom thou persecutest: it is hard for thee to kick against the pricks. And he trembling and astonished said, Lord, what wilt thou have me to do? And the Lord said unto him, Arise, and go into the city, and it shall be told thee what thou must do."

Notice the masterly skill of an Almighty God. Paul is talking about what he is going to do (boasting); get a people in authority to go along with his plan, when his plan was not the plan of God. God will allow you to get only so far outside of His plan, but it's here where Paul had fought against God's plan. He had a heart for God; he wanted to fight and guard the law, but he missed God in His Son. And while on his way to do his plan, God revealed His Son to Paul. If we are going to know Jesus it will not be through books nor will it be through what one teaches us, but it's going to be through a revelation from God. Jesus even told

Peter that the only reason that you know that I am the son of the living God is because the father revealed it to you. You walking with me did not make you know that; listening to me teach did not make you know that either, but that came from the father. A part of Paul's testimony was being thankful that God would reveal His Son to him.

Galatians 1:15,16... "But when it pleased God, who separated me from my mother's womb, and called me by his grace, To reveal his Son in me, that I might preach him among the heathen; immediately I conferred not with flesh and blood:"

So it's right here in Acts we find that against the will of Paul, God interrupts his plans and caused *His (God's)* plans to immediately go into effect. It began when Paul, because of his desire to do his own will, that he was forced to humble himself. The text said Paul immediately knew it was "Lord" (Revelation). And it wasn't until he got a revelation of who the Lord was that he was able to hear Him. If you are in a place where it appears that hearing God is becoming more complicated, then it may be possible that you may need to humble yourself or your own will is about to force you into a place of humility.

I am totally consumed by the command that God gave unto Paul. He said, "Go into the city and it shall be told thee what thou "must" do." The next assignment that Paul received before he moved into his place of destiny was given to him by a "Man of God." Yes, God could have told him while he had him down; God could have revealed it to him before going to Damascus, but God worked through His predestined plan. He used a man to tell Paul his next move. And if Paul would have chosen to not listen to the Man of God, he would have remained blind to the will that God had for his life. He had a zeal for God, and was willing to fight for what he thought was right, but he would have never reached that place in God if he would not have humbled himself to another man.

HUMBLE YOURSELF AND BE LIFTED!

Chapter Two

THE CAUSE OF YOUR AFFLICTIONS

God caused Paul to be afflicted in order to get his attention and get him into a place in which he could more effectively use him. That revelation helps us understand the Bible when it talks about the afflictions of the righteous. God knows how to deliver him out of them all. Psalms 34:19 (KJV) says, "Many are the afflictions of the righteous: but the Lord delivereth him out of them all." But the Message version said it a little differently…"Disciples so often get into trouble; still, GOD is there every time."

The only reason God will allow you to be afflicted is so that the affliction can humble you and He can lift you. Oftentimes, God has to use afflictions to humble us because we won't humble ourselves. One of the most amazing discoveries is that if we do not learn how to humble ourselves, then we will not walk in the power in which we were created to possess. Since it is God Who gives us confidence that He is able to perform and complete the work He started in us, He will afflict us to humble us.

Throughout the history of the Bible, we can notice that God would use afflictions to grow us. You have to know that you have not reached your place of destiny and it can only be accomplished through humility. If we cannot humble ourselves, God has a perfectly designed affliction waiting to humble us. It's not to make us stop; it's not to make us give up; it's not to cause us to become bitter, but it's used to perfect us. There is a quaint vignette in the body of Christ that insinuates that when a shepherd wants a disobedient sheep to follow him, he would break its leg and then carry the sheep until it is well and have learned its shepherd. That insinuates that only one sheep at a time will disobey the shepherd. It's not in the history of the shepherd that that is one of his methods of getting a wayward sheep to follow.

Now that we know that is a myth, let us look at how the Bible said it. The Bible said the sheep knows the voice of his shepherd and the sheep follow and obey the voice of the shepherd. All the shepherd does is love the sheep. It is written in the Scriptures that if a sheep is lost, the shepherd goes and find the sheep and rejoices when he finds him. This foundational truth gives new meaning to the word "afflictions." Afflictions then is when God allows you to do it your way, and allows you to find out that *your way* is not the way that God ordained it. But because you tried it your way, you got yourself in trouble, causing you to humble yourself to God so he could get you out of the trouble you got yourself in. I call this a "Prodigal Situation." It is where we have gone out on our own, done it the way we liked it, then realized that if we stayed in that place we would die, even though we had a father who has life in abundance.

All of us have "Prodigal Situations" where we will find ourselves in a place that is not conducive with who we are. Nevertheless, we have to come to ourselves and realize that we have a father who is waiting on our return.

Luke 15:11-20… "And he said, A certain man had two sons: And the younger of them said to his father, Father, give me the portion of goods that falleth to me. And he divided unto them his living. And not many days after the younger son gathered all together, and took his journey into a far country, and there wasted his substance with riotous living. And when he had spent all, there arose a mighty famine in that land; and he began to be in want. And he went and joined himself to a citizen of that country; and he sent him into his fields to feed swine. And he would fain have filled his belly with the husks that the swine did eat: and no man gave unto him. And when he came to himself, he said, How many hired servants of my father's have bread enough and to spare, and I perish with hunger! I will arise and go to my father, and will say unto him, Father, I have sinned against heaven, and before thee, And am no more worthy to be called thy son: make me as one of thy hired servants. And he arose, and came to his father. But when he was yet a great way off, his father saw him, and had compassion, and ran, and fell on his neck, and kissed him."

Look at the text...there was no broken leg. The condition was not a result of the father, and it was a place of affliction. The affliction was a result of the son's decision because he failed to remain humble. The father allowed him to do what he desired to do. And finally he realized that his way was not one that would cause the father to rejoice. And because the father loved him, there was an everyday expectancy from the father that the son would humble himself and come back to him. The text said it wasn't until he came to himself that he remembered the father. He decided to make a decision to come back to the father, repent and be restored. Remember, repent and return. God is there filled with compassion and will meet you. He will kiss you and fall on you. Every time we go astray and decide to love God again, He always kiss us and show His great compassion that is anew every day. If you are still reading this book right now, it's possible that you need a kiss from the Father. All you have to do right now is turn towards Him, arise up out of that place that you are in and go back home.

HUMBLE YOURSELF AND BE LIFTED!

Chapter Three

ALLOW PATIENCE TO WORK

God wants us to humble ourselves so that we can live the life we were created to live and become the person we were created to be, by allowing patience to have her perfect work. Patience is the very tool God uses to humble us. After we have walked after our own will as the prodigal son, we find ourselves afflicted because of our attitude. But God through patience, gives us the ability to produce whatever we need to be complete and perfect.

James 1:3,4 (KJV)…"Knowing this, that the trying of your faith worketh patience. But let patience have her perfect work, that ye may be perfect and entire, wanting nothing." But the Message Version said it like this, "You know that under pressure, your faith-life is forced into the open and shows its true colors. So don't try to get out of anything prematurely. Let it do its work so you become mature and well-developed, not deficient in any way."

My spirit was arrested with this portion of the Scriptures. When I find myself under the scrutiny of my selfish, egotistic, narcissistic attitude and desires, I put my faith in an unexpected place without knowing it. I put it in a place of testing. It is while it's being tested that it goes under pressure and starts producing patience. I like the Message Version, because it said that it forces it into the open and causes it to reveal its true colors. Now the part that handcuffed my spirit and tasered my thinking was when God, through the Spirit of God gave patience a gender! "Her" connoting the ability to carry a load, the ability to give birth, the ability to nurture and most of all through patience, "her" is the ability to love. Furthermore, when we allow it to go its full-term, it births and give life to whatever it is that we are lacking and keeping us from being entire and cause us to want nothing.

It causes us to be made whole. I found that many of us are saved and we love God, but we have not been made whole because we fail to humble ourselves. Now this is my favorite part of this book. If patience can produce what I need to be entire and lacking nothing, then I can at that point, consider myself whole. Through the process and working of the Holy Spirit, we find that those who were made whole were those who learned the art of worship. That then indicates that part of patience while it is at work pushes us into a place of worship. Patience then has a spiritual push and forces us into the presence of God. It is here when she has pushed us into the presence of God that we become mature and well-developed. It is when she pushes us into the presence of God that we become entire and not lacking, "whole." If we are going to be whole, it will require a humility that will cause us to trust God to fix us even after we have broken ourselves.

HUMBLE YOURSELF AND BE LIFTED!

Chapter Four

A REALITY CHECK OF YOUR FAITH

As we scrutinize the moments in Scriptures where one was made whole, you have to not fail to see that wholeness was always connected with one's faith. It takes a great faith to be in a place that you got yourself in, getting exactly what you deserve, while at the same time, still believing that God is working it for your good. It takes a great faith to ask God for what you know you don't deserve, and yet you are expecting Him to do it. It's this kind of faith that is connected with worship that causes God to move on your behalf. And He moves not because you changed His plan, He moved because your faith pleased Him, and he moved during a happy moment.

The reality is our faith is not designed to move God, but faith is designed to make us move. We have used our faith as a panacea to make God change His plans, when in reality, faith is only to please Him. Here is the conviction… faith pleases God but causes us to move towards God. Let's evaluate the Scriptures.

Luke 17:12-19… "And as he entered into a certain village, there met him ten men that were lepers, which stood afar off: And they lifted up their voices, and said, Jesus, Master, have mercy on us. And when he saw them, he said unto them, Go shew yourselves unto the priests. And it came to pass, that, as they went, they were cleansed. And one of them, when he saw that he was healed, turned back, and with a loud voice glorified God, And fell down on his face at his feet, giving him thanks: and he was a Samaritan. And Jesus answering said, "Were there not ten cleansed? But where are the nine? There are not found that returned to give glory to God, save this stranger. And he said unto him, Arise, go thy way: thy faith hath made thee whole."

Matthew 15:25-28… "Then came she and worshipped him, saying, Lord, help me. But he answered and said, It is not meet to take the children's bread, and to cast it to dogs. And she said, "Truth, Lord: yet the dogs eat of the crumbs which fall from their masters' table. Then Jesus answered and said unto her, O woman, great is thy faith: be it unto thee even as thou wilt. And her daughter was made whole from that very hour."

Mark 10:51,52... "And Jesus answered and said unto him, What wilt thou that I should do unto thee? The blind man said unto him, Lord, that I might receive my sight. And Jesus said unto him, Go thy way; thy faith hath made thee whole. And immediately he received his sight, and followed Jesus in the way."

Now the thing that is common in these Scriptures is the main characters had a faith that was able to sustain and hold up what they desired. And through that, they were made whole. The faith made them move and it pleased God. Faith provoked them to transition into a place of worship; it caused their posture to change. In each case you saw a worshiper, someone who was energized by their faith and pleased God. To worship and exhibit faith, you will need humility as one of your variables.

Humility is my ability to orderly place myself under someone else. Humility is a level of freedom that not many believers gets to experience. Humility is the very key that unlocks the power of God in your life. Those descriptions of humility are the same variables that are needed to worship and exhibit faith in God. Look at how it works.

Faith pleases God and He is seeking a worshipper. We are in the image of God, and for that reason I feel that many of our desires can be traced to God. When I start to seek after something, I'm going to seek after what pleases me. And if I can be pleased with faith, then I'm truly seeking after someone who has faith in me and knows how to please me. So as we rip up the text, we can then conclude that God is seeking those who will humble themselves, be motivated by their faith and by faith, be transitioned into a place of worship, finding ourselves at the feet of our Savior and Lover of our souls.

I cannot leave you thinking that you are a better worshipper than the other person, so let me suggest this to you…we are all seeking to move to the highest level of worship, which is obedience. You may have thought it was when you get to the part of the song that give you chills or when you start speaking in tongues. Better yet, you may have thought high worship was when you were in your prayer closet, interceding and bombarding Satan's kingdom. Beloved, I am writing this section to defy that philosophy and provoke a mindset to take worship to its highest level, which is simply obedience. To be humble, one must be able to obey. The choice is yours!

HUMBLE YOURSELF AND BE LIFTED!

Chapter Five

HUMILTY = OBEDIENCE

If you are going to humble yourself and not be willing to obey the person that you orderly set yourself under, then what you call being humble is not humility at all. In every act of humility, there is an act of obedience. We have applied the art of giving and offerings as our way of worship. We have allowed the scorched concept of who our God is to cause us to forfeit the true element of worship. The true element of worship or should I say the element that causes worship to be complete is obedience. God said, "It is better to obey than to offer sacrifice," (1 Samuel 15:22). You remember when Saul was given the instructions to utterly destroy the Amalekites and fight them until they were consumed or until the job was done. Now if you do what the Lord says and do not complete the command that was given, even though you did that part, but did not do it completely, then it is still disobedience. Partial obedience is total disobedience. Saul thought that he had done what the Lord had said, but he wanted to offer sacrifices to God; therefore, he did not kill all the animals. And even though he did part of what God wanted, he did not do all that God told him. Therefore, in essence, he disobeyed. Let us observe the following Scriptures:

> *1Samuel 15:3... "Now go and smite Amalek, and utterly destroy all that they have, and spare them not; but slay both man and woman, infant and suckling, ox and sheep, camel and ass."*

> *1Samuel 15: 18-23... "And the Lord sent thee on a journey, and said, Go and utterly destroy the sinners the Amalekites, and fight against them until they be consumed. Wherefore then didst thou not obey the voice of the Lord, but didst fly upon the spoil, and didst evil in the sight of the Lord? And Saul said unto Samuel, Yea, I have obeyed the voice of the Lord, and have gone the way which the Lord sent me, and have brought Agag the king of Amalek, and have utterly destroyed the Amalekites. But the people took of the spoil, sheep and oxen, the chief of the things which should have been utterly destroyed, to sacrifice unto the Lord thy God in Gilgal. And Samuel said, Hath the Lord as great delight in burnt offerings and sacrifices, as in obeying the voice of*

the Lord? Behold, to obey is better than sacrifice, and to hearken than the fat of rams. For rebellion is as the sin of witchcraft, and stubbornness is as iniquity and idolatry. Because thou hast rejected the word of the Lord, he hath also rejected thee from being king."

The highest level of worship is obedience. What we offer God and what we use in an attempt to please Him will never be greater than obeying Him. Saul wanted to offer sacrifices to God and offering sacrifices is not a bad thing because God requires a sacrifice from us. But to obey is better. To obey then is more superior, more excellent, and more effective. It exceeds sacrifice because sacrifice involves elements from your fleshly desires. Sacrifice involves you, but obedience to God involves a submission of your will to the will of God.

If you want results through worship, then we must understand the art of obedience. This word "obey" is the Hebrew word "shama" (shaw-mah') and it is most famously used to introduce the "shema." Shema is known as lines in a prayer in the morning and evening; the centerpiece of our service. This word "obedience" has a parallel usage; when the heavens are commanded to hear the prophet's message. You may not understand all of that, but here is a laymen explanation of the word "obedience." When we choose to obey God, then our obedience becomes the centerpiece to our prayer to God, and it commands the heaven to respond to what we are praying. Your prayers are not answered because you pray so well and have a lot of enticing words to say to God. But your prayers are answered because you choose to obey God. When we obey God and begin to bind and loose in the earth, our words command heaven to bind and loose also. We are simply using the keys or the authority given to us by Jesus.

Matthew 18:18-20... "Verily I say unto you, Whatsoever ye shall bind on earth shall be bound in heaven: and whatsoever ye shall loose on earth shall be loosed in heaven. Again I say unto you, That if two of you shall agree on earth as touching anything that they shall ask, it shall be done for them of my Father which is in heaven. For where two or three are gathered together in my name, there am I in the midst of them."

When I choose to obey, it's simply saying that I hear God intelligently and agree with Him and I will do what He says. When I agree with Him and do what He says, then I can ask any thing and it shall be done of the Father. And the context is "whatsoever I shall bind and loose in earth shall be bound and loose in heaven." This signifies to us that whatever we interdict or prohibit in the earth will be interdicted and prohibited in the heavens. And whatsoever you decide to release, dismiss or dissolve in the earth will be released, dismissed and dissolved in the heavens. Heaven gets it command from the disciple who will humble himself and obey the Word of God. This kind of obedience requires humility. And this humility towards God will be revealed in how I choose to obey those who God placed over my life. Or should I say who you choose to be over your life as it relates to the things of God. Characteristically, humility is the submission of our will to God's will. It comes from the Greek word, "hupotasso," meaning to place in an orderly fashion under something. In our case as believers, it's not humbling ourselves under something, but it is humbling ourselves under *someone*; submitting our wills under someone else's will. That is why it's easy to say that any believer who does not have a pastor exhibits the very first sign of pride which is the opposite of humility. Humility is always looking for someone to submit to.

HUMBLE YOURSELF AND BE LIFTED!

Chapter Six

PRIDE ≠ HUMILITY

The biggest enemy of humility is pride. Humility causes us to live the life that we were created to live because we have submitted to our call in life which was in Christ. Humility is when I have an accurate estimate of my worth. That's why the Bible said we ought not to think more highly of ourselves as we ought to think. And if we fail to give ourselves to him then our creative purpose continues to be hidden, and make us to be compelled to live the life based on the standard of others which will always be beneath the life of God. That's when pride comes in. Prides simply say that I want to do what I want to do and what I want is not subject to what God want for me. When you walk in pride then you never become and fulfill your created purpose. When we walk in pride then we become one of the people that God resist. We become one of the individuals that God will stand against and oppose. When God resists you, it prevents every effort from working.

The reason that the idea has not worked yet is because you have not yet humbled yourself. The idea you have is a God idea, but it has not worked for you because you are trying to make it *your* idea. Humble yourself if you want it to work.

HUMBLE YOURSELF AND BE LIFTED!

Chapter Seven

SUBMIT!

This is a prophetic word for you from the throne of God: "If you discuss it with your leader and not be secretive, it will work for you!"

This part of the writing may lose all of those who have not learned to walk in a spirit of humility. Humility is how we perfect our relationship with God, but we can't have a perfect relationship with God without having a perfect relationship with our leaders. Now to a humble person this will help you, but if you possess an ounce of pride, you will never be able to retain what I'm about to say. In the church, the Pastor is god. In the home, the husband is god; on the job the boss is god. The reason that they are gods is because they are the ones who are operating with the authority of God. Look, every Sheriff Deputy operates under the authority of the Sheriff. The Sheriff doesn't have to be present for the arrest to be made. In fact some nights they are home in bed and the Sheriff Deputy is out patrolling with the authority of the Sheriff; so much so that we don't call him a Sheriff Deputy, we call him the Sheriff.

Okay, you need a Scripture. Romans 13:1-2 states, "Let every soul be subject to the higher powers. For there is no power but of God: the powers that be are ordained of God. And whosoever therefore resisteth the power, resisteth the ordinance of God; And they that resist shall receive to themselves damnation."

No let me say it in laymen's terms. Every soul must submit and humble himself to the higher powers. There is no power but of God. That means it does not matter who the higher power is; it's still God's power, because there is no power but of God. Furthermore, those higher powers are powers because God ordained them, and if you resist them, then you are resisting what God has ordained, causing God to resist you. When God is resisting you, you will bring upon yourself damnation. Now to validate this even further, there is another Scripture that says whatever we do, we are to do it heartily as unto God. Somebody is still fighting this gospel, because you don't understand humility like Aaron did who understood that God made Moses his god; just as Sarah did by calling her husband Abraham, "Lord."

Your humility towards God is revealed in your humility towards your leader and one another. And if we are not humbling ourselves then we are walking in pride. Pride is the enemy of God and it's originator is the devil. It started when he decided that he wanted to be above God and not under God. When we lose respect for our leaders, then we want to be above them, and pride becomes the centerpiece of our motives and not obedience.

The antidote to never losing respect for your leader and keeping yourself in a place of humility is to always pray for those who have authority over you. It is impossible to pray for someone you have no respect for. That's why He wants us to pray for our enemies because He knows that when we pray for them, our enemies will no longer be considered our enemy. Also, if you are praying for someone who you believe is your enemy and after you have prayed, you still think they are your enemy, then you need to humble yourself, obey the Word of God and try prayer again. There may be something that needs to be bound and loosed so heaven can respond. It is even possible that you are operating in rebellion and stubbornness. Please understand beloved that your prayer will not be answered if you are operating in a prideful and disobedient spirit. Just submit!

HUMBLE YOURSELF AND BE LIFTED!

Chapter eight

THE CHOICE IS YOURS

Now when the Bible says humble yourself, it means that humility is something that you have to choose to do. It did not suggest that you pray for humility. It did not suggest that you would fast for humility, but the Bible said humble yourself. It did not suggest how; it said do it. It did not give any ideas on how it's done, but it said do it.

It's an act of your will, and is done in our spirit. Humility is the only thing we can give to God that He did not give us. Anything we offer unto the Lord is simply because He has already given it unto us. Humility, however, was not given to us by God. Yet, when we humble ourselves to Him, then we are submitting our will to Him freely. Therefore, humbling ourselves is something we have to do ourselves. The secret to humility is obedience. But when we are not obedient, then we will find ourselves in rebellion and stubbornness or under the power of witchcraft and idolatry. Witchcraft is described as a sin, therefore, it can also be described as a creature ready to pounce, lurking at the doors of the disobedient and proud heart.

> *1 Peter 5:5,6… "Likewise, ye younger, submit yourselves unto the elder. Yea, all of you be subject one to another, and be clothed with humility: for God resisteth the proud, and giveth grace to the humble. Humble yourselves therefore under the mighty hand of God, that he may exalt you in due time:"*

This passage reveals the hypocrisy of many believers. It reveals to us when we choose not to be subject one to another and do not cloth ourselves with humility, God then becomes our enemy. However, we attempt to use our faith as a magic potion to change God's mind and how He feels concerning our behavior. The passage declared we are to be clothed with humility, but in Greek language, the grammatical subtext is the Aorist imperative which denotes a command for doing something in the future that is a simple action. In simplest terminology, we should choose this one basic action because God resists the proud, but giveth grace to the humble. That modestly means God is continually empowering the disciple who humbles himself.

God resists the proud and this should be our reason to humble ourselves under the mighty hand of God and in due time, He will lift us. Humility is when I put myself under God and His mighty hand. When I'm under something, that means what I'm under is over me, and I have to be able to bear the weight of what I'm under. If I remain under it, then when it moves, it will move up and not around. When I am under the hand of God and if I choose to remain under the hand of God, then when God moves He moves up; and when God moves up, it is my responsibility to move up also to remain under His hand.

This section of the book is a special treat! At this point, you should be experiencing a level of conviction and expectancy. There is absolutely no way you have not found yourself amid these pages and it is only because God loves you. If you have placed yourself under God and you can't feel His touch, it is because He is calling you higher. He is giving you room to grow and expand; He is preparing and setting you up for a Jabez blessing.

1 Chronicles 4:10… "And Jabez called on the God of Israel, saying, Oh that thou wouldest bless me indeed, and enlarge my coast, and that thine hand might be with me, and that thou wouldest keep me from evil, that it may not grieve me! And God granted him that which he requested.

This is the kind of blessing that can only come by the hand of God. It is the kind of blessing where God will stretch us through humility and prepare us for more grace, protect us from the grievance of evil and grant our request. This happens only by God's hand and when we decide that we are going to humble ourselves. It happens when we decide to give God the one thing that He asks for, even though it belongs to us. God created us and gave us everything, yet He didn't give us humility. Humility is when I know I have been given the power to rule, but I choose to be ruled by the one thing greater than me, God. When I choose to be ruled by the one thing that is greater than me, then I'm allowing the greater to be my Lord. I chose to give up my rights to be who I am, so that I could be a direct resemblance and an ambassador of the one who I freely gave my rights, authority, and my will to…God.

HUMBLE YOURSELF AND BE LIFTED!

Chapter Nine

Don't Fool Yourself

As noted in an earlier chapter, when the Bible says to humble yourself under the mighty hand of God, God is saying, "Place yourself and your will under My will." This means we should fashion our wills after the will of God. Humility is when I have an accurate estimate or assessment of my worth. That's why the Bible said we ought not to think more highly of ourselves as we ought to think. Being humble means that there must be an awareness within you to know who you are and who it is that you belong. When you are aware of that, you don't have to exalt yourself because self-exaltation is the recipe for humiliation.

Please note there is a difference between humility and humiliation. First, humiliation is always connected with your ego. It forces a negative difference between who you want to be and who you truly are. It becomes a negative difference when my ego generates a false image of who I am and it detaches me from who I really am. Therefore, it is when I'm trying to be who I'm not that causes humiliation to be conceived.

Humility, on the other hand, occurs proactively when you loosen attachment to your ego and have a sober look at who you are. Regardless of the place and situation that you may find yourself in, I have concluded that if you humble yourself while in it, you won't have to deal with the humiliation of it. You will not have to deal with the "Rich Man Syndrome." The rich man would not have had to deal with the humiliation he dealt with if he would have humbled himself in the sight of God (Luke 16:20-30). The rich man had to deal with the humiliation of hell because he would not humble himself, while the poor beggar found himself in the comfort of God (Ref. Ephesians 5:21…Submitting yourselves one to another in the fear of God).

You had to deal with the humiliation of the divorce because you would not humble yourself; We are forced to deal with the humiliations in life; i.e. divorce, loss of job, home, car or relationship, because we fail to humble ourselves. In every place in life where there was humiliation, there was also an opportunity for humility. Because a dose of humility counteracts the poison of humiliation. It is impossible to embrace an opportunity for pride and not also have the opportunity for humility. But what occurs is we naturally offer pride because pride gives us permission to want to be better than someone else. In the same manner that we were conceived in sin, pride became a part of our nature and is wired into us; therefore all that is required is an opportunity. God did not give us humility but He asks us for it; and the only possible way we can give Him what He did not give us is when we choose to obey Him. It's that act of obedience that causes Him to not withhold anything from us.

The reason that God wants us to humble ourselves is so that He can give us gifts. When we humble ourselves under the mighty hand of God, since the gifts come from above, then we are already in position to receive. Let us scrutinize James 1:17 (KJV).

James 1:17..."Every good gift and every perfect gift is from above, and cometh down from the Father of lights, with whom is no variableness, neither shadow of turning."

This verse tells us a few things. First of all, it tells us where every good gift and every perfect gift comes from. This text talks about a good gift and a perfect gift; however, the word "gift" carries different mechanics in its use. One mechanic of the word is the act of giving, and the next use of the word means "to bestow." It is God that gives and bestows upon us. Therefore, what makes the gifts good and perfect is that they benefit and mature us. But do not err! What God gives us is not what makes us great or greater. If you look at the grammar in the text, it causes a shifting in the gifting. The writer adds the conjunction "and". This conjunction causes the gift to shift; it shifts from its place of origin to its place of dwelling. The text said, "They come down." This is why it's important for us to be under God because what we need to benefit us and to mature us comes down from God (the Father of Lights). It is gravitational pull which causes something to come straight down. When the oil was poured on the head, it came down upon the beard. That's because of the pull of gravity, causing the oil to smear everything that's under it. So it is with the gifts of God; the gravitational pull causes them to fall on those who are under Him. *Variableness* and *shadow of turning* speaks of the light. When we examine the analogy of the sun, we have to acknowledge the fact that nothing can stop the sun from being the sun and nothing can stop it from shining. When it is cloudy, the sun is still shining; when it's raining the sun is still shining; nothing can stop the sun from shining. But there are things that can obstruct the brightness of the sun, causing us to think that it is not shining. God is in essence the very same. Nothing can stop Him from being God. There is no place we can go and He not be God, but there are some things that will cause us to think that God is not God. Conclusively, it is when we fail to humble ourselves. As a consequence, we then have to deal with the resistance of God.

HUMBLE YOURSELF AND BE LIFTED!

CHAPTER TEN

THE SECRET TO GREATNESS

Every blood bought, blood washed born again believer have an inward inclination to be great. That inclination comes from knowing who your God is and because we have been created in His image and prized above all of His creation. Oftentimes, we miss the most important variable for greatness, and that is humility. In the following passage of Scripture, observe how the disciples humiliated themselves by going to Jesus, jocking for positions in the kingdom and asking who was the greatest in the kingdom.

Matthew 18:1-3... "At the same time came the disciples unto Jesus, saying, Who is the greatest in the kingdom of heaven? And Jesus called a little child unto him, and set him in the midst of them, And said, Verily I say unto you,

Except ye be converted, and become as little children, ye shall not enter into the kingdom of heaven."

Look at how Jesus responded. He took this little child and placed him in the middle of them, and said, "Except you be converted and become as little children you shall not see the kingdom." Jesus said you won't even see it which is much less than being great in it.

"But whosoever will humble himself as this little child is the greatest." This right here is for all those who want to be great, but haven't arrived yet. If you are going to be great, the first thing you have to do is be converted. Until I studied this, I could not understand why it was so hard for veteran Christians to humble themselves, and the answer was in the text…because they still have not been converted. They got save, but did not convert. They received the Holy Ghost, but did not convert. They have been in the church for a very long time, but they still have not converted.

This is just for the first thousand to read this book, and who really want to be great. You have to be converted to a child! An obedient child never rises above his parents and when the child leaves, he does it with permission. When a child wants a snack out of the refrigerator, he asks the parent. If a child wants to go somewhere, they will ask the parent and remain in the range of a scream. Lastly, a child is in the house at the time he's told. But every rebellious child who starts breaking the rules of the house gets disciplined in the house and if the correction does not work, then he gets put out of the house. God said if you really want to be great, learn how to submit to leadership like an obedient child submits to his parent.

Wait; I want to make a mature Christian shout! When you are converted, you don't go days and weeks mad at one another. Children can fight now and be pushing each other in a swing ten minutes later. But sadly, we have fire baptized, blood bought and blood washed born again believers who will fight each other for weeks, months and years, because they refuse to be converted and humble themselves.

HUMBLE YOURSELF AND BE LIFTED!

CHAPTER ELEVEN

MIRROR OR WINDOW?

Being converted gives us the power to be humble because it causes us to look through God's spiritual windows and not into the mirror of selfishness. Being converted is the same as being transformed.

Romans 12:1-3... "I beseech you therefore, brethren, by the mercies of God, that ye present your bodies a living sacrifice, holy, acceptable unto God, which is your reasonable service. And be not conformed to this world: but be ye transformed by the renewing of your mind, that ye may prove what is that good, and acceptable, and perfect, will of God. For I say, through the grace given unto me, to every man that is among you, not to think of himself more highly than he ought to think; but to think soberly, according as God hath dealt to every man the measure of faith."

This text starts out compelling us to give and present ourselves unto the Lord. Presenting yourself to God is the same as humbling yourself *under* God. When you submit to God, you are actually presenting yourself to Him for the approval to go higher. When you present yourself to God, then you can be converted.

For those of you who want to be free but haven't figured it out yet, here it is. I began this chapter talking about a mirror and a window. They are important because they have different functions as it relates to your walk and attitude. The mirror causes you to be conformed, but the window causes you to be transformed. The mirror puts your focus on you, but the window helps you focus on others. When you start looking through the window, you become a mirror to God. God begins to look at you and see an image of Himself. If you are going to be a mirror to God, you have to learn how to give yourself to the things and assignments of God, which is people. Each and every one of us has been assigned to serve one another. God not only wants you to look through the window, but He wants to make you a window. God wants to shine his light through you so someone can look at you and see their future being brighter than their current dark situation.

When we look into the spiritual windows that God puts before us, it keeps us from thinking more highly of ourselves than we ought to think.

In Romans 12:1-3, we must pay close attention to its grammar. It said, "…Through the grace given to me and to those that is among me, to not think more highly of ourselves than we ought to think." This text did not say that we should not think high of ourselves, but it did say that we should not think *more* highly than we ought to think. That simply means that I have to be completely honest with myself and about who I am. When you start thinking of yourself, you have to do it with some sobriety. Don't allow your mind to be drunken with pride. Don't allow your mind to be blinded by the deceitfulness of riches, but think soberly. And when you think about who you are in a sober manner, you will also realize that pride can come in unaware and you may not be as humble as you thought you were. If we are going to allow God to look at us and see Himself in us, then we have to humble ourselves and submit to one another as the Scripture has commanded.

HUMBLE YOURSELF AND BE LIFTED!

CHAPTER TWELVE

WHERE DO YOU STAND?

This chapter is designed to reveal your true level of humility. You say you are humble; you say that He is your all and all, but the only way God can see Himself in you and the image of His Son formed in you is when you allow God to make you a window. Somebody say, "Bishop if you don't take long, I'll let you tell me how He can make me a window."

"Bring ye all the tithes into the storehouse, that there may be meat in mine house, and prove me now herewith, saith the Lord of hosts, if I will not open you the windows of heaven, and pour you out a blessing, that there shall not be room enough to receive it." (Malachi 3:10)

Giving is one of the most vivid indications of humility. If we humble ourselves in the sight of God and God sees how we give, the Scripture said He will open us and pour us out. If you are a tither and giver, allow me to dissect the text real quickly, and it should cause you to want to give more. The text said that if you would bring all the tithes into the storehouse, that there may be meat in mine house and prove me now herewith. Prove me with the tithe; don't prove with the prayer. Don't prove me with your fasting; don't prove me with your offering, but prove me with your tithe.

Let's continue to follow the passage. This part is for the excellent grammar students. The text goes on further to say, "…if I will not open you." The subject of the matter is *you*; and He wants to do something to you. The "window of heaven" is a prepositional phrase that describes the subject, which is you. So God is not trying to open the window of heaven; He is trying to open you. And make you to become the window. Don't you get it? When He makes you a window, then He pours Himself through you. He will pour you on folks where they won't be able to receive all of the love that God wants to love them with. This text clearly tells us that the love will come in the form of blessings. He wants to open you and pour you, but it can only happen when you learn how to humble yourself. If He opens you,

He makes you a window. But, if He pours you, He makes you a blessing. Therefore, when you are humble, you are either a window or a blessing at all times; and when you are a window, then you become God's mirror and the blessing that He desires to pour out onto others.

Allow me to bring the book to a conclusion by saying this. You have to be like the master. If you want to fulfill the joy of God, then you have to be likeminded and have the same love, while with one accord and one mind. Humble yourself and let nothing be done through strife or vainglory. Put glory in the right place and with a lowliness of mind, esteem others better than yourself. Look through the window like Jesus did.

Don't look on your own things, but on the things of others He was in the form of God, but thought it not robbery to be equal with God: He didn't make reputation of himself; and He took on the form of a servant and the likeness of men: And being found in fashion as a man, He humbled Himself, and became obedient unto death. And because of his obedience God highly exalted him and gave Him a name that is above every name. (Philippians 2:4-7)

If you want your name to be great, you have to be converted and humble yourself. The text said, "At his name every knee should bow, and that every tongue should confess that Jesus Christ is Lord, to the glory of God the Father." (Philippians 2:10-11) Humble yourself, work out your salvation and watch God work in you, both to will and to do of his good pleasure. Humble yourself and do it without a murmur or dispute; humble yourself and be blameless and harmless; humble yourself so that you will be without rebuke and called a son of God. (Philippians 2:12-13)

Humble yourself and shine as lights in the world. That is what Jesus did. He humbled Himself and became the light of the world. He humbled Himself and God lifted Him high above the enemy. Therefore, if God opens doors and blesses you, stay humble. If you have to suffer lack, stay humble. When you start to walk in your abundance, stay humble. Regardless of where you are, be content and remain humble like your teacher, Jesus. They crucified Him and he remained humble. They whipped Him from the sixth to ninth hours, yet He remained humble. They pierced His side and put a crown of thorns on His head, but he stayed humble. The Bible said they put Him in the grave and on the third day, He was highly exalted by the Father. Stay humble; God is trying to lift you up.

HUMBLE YOURSELF AND BE LIFTED!

ABOUT THE AUTHOR

Bishop Clifton Junior Staton

Bishop Dr. Clifton J. Staton is a native of Bethel, North Carolina and the oldest of 16 siblings. Bishop Dr. Staton attended and graduated from the Pitt County Public School System. After graduation, he enlisted and served faithfully in the Unites States Marine Corps. He later attended Martin Community College and received his certification and became a certified electrician and started his successful business, CJS Electricals.

Bishop Dr. Staton has been married to Minister Paulette Staton for 27 years and to this union they have two sons; Clifton Staton Jr. and Terrill Staton (Sybil) and one daughter Chantel Staton. His family is his driving force in life and it's his most earnest prayer to allow the glory of God to be revealed through his family.

Bishop Dr. Staton answered the call and was baptized in 1994 at the age of 28. In 1995, he preached his first message under the ministries, leadership and tutelage of Elder Charles Staton of the Full Gospel Tabernacle Holiness Church in Bethel, NC. Several years later He was inspired by the Spirit of God to submit his ministry and giftings under the ministry of Pastor Gregory Black of St. John Missionary Baptist Church in Stokes, NC. At both ministries combined he served in the choir, deacon ministry, associate minister and First vice of Youth Auxiliary in Middle Ground Union.

In May 2002, he completed and received his Bachelor Degree. In 2003, he was ordained as the pastor and overseer of Rhema Word Ministries at St. Paul Missionary

Baptist Church in Oak City, N.C. In August 2016, he accepted the call and was consecrated to the office of Bishop. In that same year, he completed his studies and received his Doctoral degree from St. Augustine Theological Institute. He also established a minority male mentoring program entitled "Impact". Through this mentoring program, the Earth Shakers Men Fellowship was established. He continues to expand the program by incorporating CIA (Christ in Action).

Bishop Dr. Staton has become one of God's most innovative speakers. Through humor, practical insight, and "down home" approaches, he delivers a refreshing Word that will challenge, strengthen and encourage God's people. He maintains a zeal and desire to continue in the development and maturity of God's eternal Word while at the same time remaining the least among many.

www.ingramcontent.com/pod-product-compliance
Lightning Source LLC
Chambersburg PA
CBHW051706090426
42736CB00013B/2568